"Working Smarter" Tips and Principles

How to Work Less and Earn more Money "Working Smarter" Tips and Principles

James Leroy Nesbitt

Share the Wealth and Grow
www.jlnesbitt.com

"Working Smarter" Tips and Principles

COPYRIGHT 2016

All rights reserved, no part of this book may be published without written permission of the publisher

Share the Wealth and Grow
www.jlnesbitt.com

"Working Smarter" Tips and Principles

You + working SMARTER = YOU ARE MORE PRODUCTIVE EARN MORE $$$$$

MORE

Share the Wealth and Grow
www.jlnesbitt.com

"Working Smarter" Tips and Principles

MORE   MONEY   EQUALS

A BETTER QUALITY OF LIFE &
MORE TIME WITH YOUR FAMILY

"Working Smarter" Tips and Principles

How to work less and earn more MONEY

Content

CHAPTER 1
WHAT IS WORKING SMARTER

CHAPTER 2
"WORKING SMARTER" PRINCIPLES

A - EFFICIENCY PRINCIPLES
B - PRIORITY PRINCIPLES
C - DELEGATING PRINCIPLES

CHAPTER 3
WORKING SMARTER -

D- AUTOMATION PRINCIPLES
E- CUT OUT DISTRACTIONS PRINCIPLES
F- MONEY MAKING PRINCIPLES

Share the Wealth and Grow
www.jlnesbitt.com

CHAPTER 4

TOOLS TO WORK SMARTER

TO DO LIST

APPS

TIMERS when and where to use them.

FILE SHARING TOOLS

CHAPTER 5

How to connect with CLIENTS ON LinkedIn

CHAPTER 6

A Short Story

"It's better to own-half a watermelon than a whole grape"

WORKING SMARTER CHECKLIST

CONCLUSION

QUOTES

Your Note pages

Share the Wealth and Grow
www.jlnesbitt.com

"Working Smarter" Tips and Principles

Chapter 1
What Is Working Smarter?

You've probably heard it a thousand times: "Work Smarter - Not Harder", but what does that actually mean? It sounds good, doesn't it? Anything that has us working less has got to be a good thing. And it is.

Working smarter means working more efficiently and getting things done in less time. Now that doesn't mean you have to run yourself ragged and work at super-speed all the time. You can't keep that up for long. If you're pushing yourself too hard, you'll eventually start to burn out. That's not what we're after here and it is definitely not working smarter.

Before we move into what exactly working smarter will accomplish, let's take a look at why it is important to focus on it. There are quite a few benefits to working smarter instead of harder. The biggest one is that you'll end up making more money per hour when working on your business. That gives you some interesting options. You can spend less time in the office and more time with your loved ones. Or you can turn around and "reinvest" that time into growing your business. It's all up to you. Most importantly it will make you feel like you're making progress and moving forward. It'll keep work fun and interesting. And it will keep you from burning yourself out as we already discussed.

Working Smarter still seems like a bit of an elusive term. Let's take a look at what it may mean to work smarter, not harder. Working Smarter Means Working More Efficiently

Have you heard of Parkinson's Law? It states that "work expands so as to fill the time available for its completion". That means it is up to you to control the time you set aside for each task. Working smarter in this case means paying attention to how long things take you and working efficiently.

Working Smarter Means Picking High Priority Tasks

You're the boss of your business. That means you're in charge of making decisions. Your most important job is to recognize and focus on high priority tasks. What can you do today that will move your business forward and improve the bottom line? Working smarter in this case means picking the right things to work on.

Working Smarter Means Delegating Some Tasks

You may start out as a one man / one-woman show, but there comes a time when you'll need some help. As your business grows there's more to be done and you're the one focusing on the high priority tasks. Efficiency only gets you so far. Working smarter in this case means realizing it's time to hire a V A [VIRTUAL ASISSTANT] or some part-time help in the shop.

Working Smarter Means Automating Some Tasks

There's some amazing software, apps and tools out there that can make your life easier. They can also save you a lot of time that you can use wisely elsewhere. Working smarter in this case means rethinking how your processes work and being open to the idea of automation.

Working Smarter Means Cutting Out Distractions

Have you ever been trying hard to finish a project by a looming deadline, only to be interrupted every 5 minutes? Of course you have… we've all been there. It can be maddening. If that slows you down, so do all the little daily interruptions we take for granted. Things like your computer or phone alerting you to a new email, checking Facebook to see what's been going on, the phone ringing or your mom stopping by for coffee and a chat since you're "working from home". Working smarter in this case means cutting out or at least minimizing distractions as much as possible during work hours.

Working Smarter Means Focusing On Money Making Tasks

Last but not least let's talk hard, cold cash. That's why we're in this… to make money. We're not always good at keeping our eye on the prize though. It's easy to get into a routine at work and do stuff, just because that's how we do it. We get the ad in the yellow pages, we write the weekly newsletter column, we attend the local chamber of commerce meeting, we move through the paces and don't stop to do the math and figure out if this is actually the most valuable use of our time and resources. Working smarter in this case means taking a long hard look at what is making us money and what isn't.

You get the idea of what working smart not hard is all about. We'll go into a lot more detail on what you can do day in and day out to work smarter in the next two sections of this book. It's easy to see that this is very different from "just" working harder. Yes, you'll still be working and getting a lot of stuff done. The big difference is that working smarter means you think about what you're doing and are making smart choices instead of putting your nose to the grindstone and knocking out random things that need doing.

Your workday will fill up with whatever you let it fill up. Don't you want to make smart choices and work on the tasks that will move you and your business forward instead of filling it with busy work? Great let's get started and move into the "Working Smarter Tips & Principles".

CHAPTER 2

"Work Smarter" Principles

Now that you have a pretty good idea of what working smarter entails, let's get into the nitty gritty details of it. This is the hands-on action where you'll find my best tips and principles to stay productive and work smart.

There's a lot of information here and a lot of different tips and principles for you to try. Don't expect every single tip or principle to work for you. Instead I suggest you give everything a try and then implement those that work best for you.

To make it a little easier to keep track, I've broken the principles down into different categories. Mix and match as you see fit and make it work. If it saves you time and effort, use it. If it doesn't, move on to another principle or try a different tip.

Let's start with a few tips on working more efficiently and getting more done in less time.

Working Smarter – Efficiency Principles

I like the idea of spending less time working and more time playing. And that's all about being efficient and making the most of the time you spend working. It also means giving it 100% when you sit down to get something done. It's not always easy and does take some practice. It's well worth it though in the end and there are some little principles you can implement that make staying on task easier.

To Do Lists Are Your Friend!!!!

My first principle is to always use a to-do list. Make it out the day before, so you can grab your coffee, sit down and get right to work in the mornings. I always try to make a list of the top 5 things I need to do the next day. I try to make this list just before I go to bed. So that I don't have to think about where to start the next morning. I keep a pen and pad on my night stand so I can make out this short list. This helps me and allows me to go to sleep. I know that there is will be no wasted time the next morning trying to figure out what I should be doing first. Now I still have my daily to do list that I create as I work through my day making a list of to do things. The list I make just before I go to sleep is my top five, being truthful sometimes I have to adjust the list. But this little tip I received from a book many years ago. Has been a something that has worked for me in working smarter and helping earn more money every day.

Having the list and knowing what you need to get accomplished, makes you work faster and get it done. Break bigger projects down into multiple list items. For example, instead of using "publish a blog post" on the to do list, break it down into smaller, more manageable steps like this:

- Choose a Blog Post Topic

- Create an Outline
- Write The Blog Post
- Format The Post
- Create an Image
- Publish The Post
- Share The Post On Social Media

Each of these smaller tasks seems a lot more doable, doesn't it?

Breaking it down also helps with time management. Let's say you have 15 minutes before your next meeting (or before you have to go pick up the kids from school). You don't have time to write and publish a blog post, but you do have time to pick a topic and write a quick outline. You can get that done, check it of the to-do list and wrap up the rest when you get back.

You can use a little notepad and pen for your to-do list, or use a phone app. I'll share some apps I've found helpful in the tools section later on in the book.

I recommend you start a new daily list. Even if you didn't get to everything yesterday, go ahead and write up a new list and transpose the items leftover to the new list. It looks less cluttered and overwhelming than a perpetual list.

Do your best to get everything done on your list each day. Push hard to cross every single item off the list. Yes, there will be times when that's not possible because you're waiting on other people, or an emergency arises during the day. Your goal each day should be to cross every item of the list. It's a great feeling when you get it all done.

Set Yourself Time Limits - Use That Kitchen Timer

I mentioned Parkinson's Law earlier. If you let it, the things on your to-do list will take you all day… even if you only wrote down 3 things. It's the nature of the beast. In order to be truly efficient, we not only need to know what we should be doing, we also need a time-frame to work in.

"Working Smarter" Tips and Principles

This is where a timer comes in handy. Grab the old kitchen timer or set a countdown alarm on your phone. Set it and get to work. It's amazing what you can get done in 15 - 30 minutes with some focus, pressure and no distractions. That article that used to take you 4 hours to write is suddenly done in 20 minutes.

Give it a try. Pick each item on your to-do list and figure out how long it should take you to get it done. Set the timer, get to work and see if you can finish early. If so, shorten the amount of time next go around. Before you know it, you'll be working faster than you ever thought possible.

Work 25 Minutes, Take a 5-minute Break.

Obviously this kind of pace isn't sustainable for hours and hours at a time. Instead, aim to work hard for 25 minutes at a time, then get up and take a break. Spend the next 5 minutes to move around, get some air, get some water and just relax for a bit before your next little "work sprint".

Also don't expect to work this hard for 8 to 10 hours a day. Yes, it can be done in a pinch, but you end up burning out. Instead, I recommend you figure out your most productive time of the day. It's different for all of us. I'm most productive between 8am and noon. That's when I work with my to-do list and timer in 25 minute highly productive intervals. That's when the bulk of my work and anything "hard" gets done.

I give myself from noon to 2pm to wrap things up and then either take the rest of the day off or play around with a little social media or research as family time permits.

Pay attention to when you do your best work. What time of the day do things seem to flow effortlessly? It may be early in the morning, or late at night. Find that time slot and schedule some super-productive work during those hours.

Work Hard, Then Play

It's not easy to stay motivated to work this hard. It's much easier to just sit at the computer for a few hours doing busy work, looking around on Facebook, doing "research" … you know the kind of stuff I'm talking about.

To stay motivated to work hard, bribe yourself with some little rewards. This could be laying on the couch watching Netflix for an hour after everything on the to-do list got done. Or being able to meet a friend for lunch (or coffee) if you get through the first 3 items on your list.

Find some things you enjoy doing and then bribe yourself with some time to do them if you get done with the hard part of your work day. It could even be a work related reward. Make yourself write that blog post before you can go play with the new image software you ordered.

Working Smarter - Priority Principles

So far we've talked about working efficiently and getting a lot done in a short amount of time. Now let's take a look at what exactly you should be working on. Being able to prioritize on the most important stuff that will have the biggest impact on your bottom line is another important skill... and I have some principles to help you figure that out.

Get The Big Picture - Map It Out

Figuring out what you should be working on can be a hard thing to do. You're in the middle of your business and busy working on whatever needs doing. As long as you're focusing on the nitty gritty, it's hard to get the big picture.

"Working Smarter" Tips and Principles

Take a few minutes every once in a while and step back. I find it helps to map things out. I get a notepad, but you could also use a big sheet of construction paper or even a white wall. Map out each part of your business and each sales process.

By getting it all out on paper you get a new perspective of how things are working and what you should be focusing on. If you're not a visual learner, try explaining how your business works to someone else.

Hiring a business coach or joining a mastermind group is another good strategy. Sometimes it takes a fresh set of eyes to point out what you should be focusing on next. Yes, hiring a coach is an added expense but if it helps you take your business to the next level and make it more profitable, it's money well spent.

Tweak The To-Do List!!!

Once you know what you should be working on next and where you should be spending most of your time, energy and money, it's time to revisit the to-do list. Make sure you set aside a big chunk of time each day to work on the things you need to do to grow your business and make it more profitable.

Use what you've already learned about making your to-do list. Break those new projects down and work your way through them from idea to profit.

When you first start to take a look at the big picture of your business, you may get all sorts of great ideas for things you can do to improve / tweak and grow. All sorts of projects big and small will popup. You may be tempted to tackle them all at once - please don't!

Instead pick one project or idea. I like for it to be something I can implement relatively quickly. It also helps to make it something where you'll see a financial return right away. For example, you may have an idea for bundling a few of your existing eBooks combining them with an offer for group coaching. The hard work of creating the info products is already done and it's just a matter of bundling things up, setting up the coaching and crafting a sales page. It's the kind of project you can knock out in just a couple of days. Go for something like that. Not only will you see progress quickly, which is nice to keep you motivated. It also brings in extra cash that you can reinvest and use to outsource some of the work on bigger projects.

Back to the main point. Pick a project, break it down into to-do list items and see it through start to finish before moving on to the next improvement. You'll see results much faster this way than starting 5 different projects and working a little here and there on them.

Work On Your Top 3 Tasks First

"Working Smarter" Tips and Principles

Here's another great productivity principle. As you're making out your to-do list for the day, write down your top 3 tasks for the day first. These are the things that need to get done and have the biggest impact on your bottom line.

Sending out an email to your customers about your latest product would be a great example of something that should be at the top of your list.

Think of it this way. What three things do you need to get done so if something happens and you can't get anything else done you'd still make progress and feel productive?

Hint - these should probably be money making tasks.

Save The Easy Stuff for Downtime

We all have things that need doing each day, but (a) aren't very hard to do and (b) don't really do much for your bottom line. Social stuff comes to mind, or approving comments on your blog. Or maybe it's hanging out on a couple of forums to connect with potential customers. We all have things like that we do every day. They help us grow our reach over time, but don't have quite the same impact as writing an epic blog post or emailing our lists.

We need to do these tasks, but they aren't things that take a lot of concentration. Save those tasks for later in the day, or whenever you have just a few minutes here and there between meetings to work on.

See how much of this type of work you can do from your smart phone. Then find those little pockets of time throughout your day. Go to Pinterest while you're drinking coffee in the morning and interact on Facebook while you're waiting in line at the grocery store or the pickup line at school. It's amazing how much you can get done in those little pockets of downtime.

Implement some of these tips and watch your productivity go through the roof.

Working Smarter - Delegating Principles

Let's get real here for a minute. No matter how productive you are and how many hours per day you work, you'll get to a point where you just can't possibly do any more - or maybe you just don't want to work 80+ hours per week for years to come.

That means it's time to start delegating. But what should you be delegating? Here are four principles to help you figure that out.

Is This the Best Use of Your Time

Think about each thing you do on a daily or weekly basis. Some things are a better use of your time than others. They make you money and help you grow your business. Other things need to be done, but aren't necessarily the best use of your time. They are the first things you want to delegate. It makes sense to hire someone to help you with that type of work, so you can focus on what brings in more cash.

Start by making a list of things you do. Then put a value next to it. I like to use 1 - 5. If something I do makes me money it gets a 5. If it's something that's basic maintenance that needs to be done but doesn't generate income, it's a 1. Everything else falls somewhere in between.

Once you have your list, you should have a pretty good idea of what you should be spending most of your time on.

Can Someone Else Do It Better and Faster?

A second way to look at this is how good are you at certain tasks. Is there someone else that can do it better and faster than you?

Maybe you dabble a bit in graphic design and while you can design your next book cover, it takes you forever and while the end result may be decent, it isn't a professional cover. Knowing how to do everything from start to finish is great and it certainly helps in the beginning when you're strapped for cash. But there comes a time when you should pass that work on to someone else.

You don't want to be the bottleneck in your product creation process. You could be focusing on marketing your book and getting it out there instead of worrying about things like graphic design and editing.

Find what you're good at and where you make the biggest difference. Then work your way towards outsourcing everything you're either not good at, or that you don't enjoy.

Starting to Outsource

Once you have an idea of what you should be working on, it's time to find other ways to get them done. We'll talk about automation in a bit, but things that need a personal touch are best outsourced.

Start by picking one thing that's holding you back right now. What's keeping you from launching that new product, publishing that book or getting in touch with a whole new segment of your target audience? Is it writing copy? Creating a pretty graphic?

Pinpoint the bottleneck and then go out and look for the right person for the job. Ask for recommendations from your peers. Take a look at outsourcing sites like ODesk, or VA Facebook groups. For quick and easy jobs, don't forget to check out Fiverr.com. I've found some great people to work with there.

Don't get discouraged if you don't find the perfect person right away. Not every outsourcer will be a good fit for you and your business. Be patient, expect lots of questions and if things don't work out, move on to someone else.

Before you know it, you'll have a great team of experts you can rely on to get the job done. It's a good feeling to know you have a go-to person whenever you need a graphic designed or a press release written.

This type of outsourcing is very flexible. You just send out and pay for the work you need done and move on to doing the rest on your own. You can spend as much or as little as you can afford to get the most critical things done and grow your business.

Hiring A - V A [Virtual Assistant]

Eventually you'll reach a point where even outsourcing some tasks isn't quite enough. You need a dedicated person to help you stay on top of every-day tasks. This could be handling your email and meeting schedule, taking care of social media postings, answer the phone, make appointments for you etc.

That's when it's time to look for a good VA or Virtual Assistant. This could be a full-time employee, or an independent contractor that you pay either hourly, by project or keep on retainer. Virtual assistants have all sorts of different skillsets and like with any other outsourcing job, it's not all that easy to find one that's a good fit.

Ask for recommendations both from other small business owners and some of the outsourcers you've been working with. When you find the right person to help you run your business you'll be amazed at how much smoother things run. Of course it also doesn't hurt the bottom line when you can focus all your time and attention on money making tasks. A well-paid VA can actually help you make more.

CHAPTER 3
Working Smarter - Automation Principles

Another great way to shorten your workload is to automate as much as possible. It's easy to get stuck in a rut of doing something a certain way. We're comfortable with the process and don't feel the need to change because it makes us feel like we're working.

Is There an Easier Way?

You can save yourself a lot of time and aggravation just by asking yourself if there's an easier way to do things. Just because you've always manually approved comments or had customers email you questions or tips to include in your next newsletter doesn't mean that's the best and easiest way to do things.

Look at how your competitors are running things. Do you see easier ways to do the same thing (or something similar to what) you're doing?

Is there a Tool / App for That?

Technology is an amazing thing and there are all sorts of tools and apps out there that make running our businesses quicker and easier. Setting up and editing an HTML website used to be a big deal. There was a huge learning curve or you needed to hire a web designer. Software like WordPress changed all that. You wouldn't think to use straight html on your website these days.

The same is true with other daily tasks. Look around and see if there are tools or apps that could make your daily tasks quicker, easier or eliminate them altogether.

Look at What Others in Your Niche or Business Model Are Automating

We already touched on this, but my favorite way to find new ways to automate is to spy on my competition. What are they using? Some of it you may see on their website, in the way they run their mailing lists, shopping carts and social media postings.

When it comes to background processes, having a chat over a couple of drinks at a local meet up or conference is always a good idea. Talking to your peers and business owners in person is one of the most valuable things you can do at a marketing conference. Pick their brain and see what you can implement for yourself and your own business.

Give automation a try. Even just a few minutes saved here and there will add up. Not having to keep up with simple little tasks also frees up brain space that you can then use to plot and plan your next big project.

Working Smarter – Tips to Cut Out Distractions

Let's keep this section short and to the point. I have four TIPS for you that will help you cut out distractions and get more work done in less time. Let's go:

Shut The Door

I don't have to tell you that you get a lot more done in a short amount of time if your thought processes aren't constantly interrupted. To make sure that doesn't happen, find a room with a door you can shut. A dedicated office is nice, but the bedroom or dining room will do for now. Let everyone know that you're off to work. If family is around, I find it also helps to let them know about how long you plan on being gone.

Ask them not to disrupt you for the next 2 hours for example, so you can sit down and finish that report you need to get done. We already talked about how setting a time limit helps us get things done faster. Not having someone come in and ask you what's for dinner tonight is also extremely helpful.

Turn Off Alerts, Alarms and Your Phone

While you're at it, go ahead and turn off your phone and any alerts or alarms you may have on your computer. Don't even get tempted by "You've got Mail" alert messages. Turn off your email program and silence your phone if turning it off isn't an option.

The only alarm that's allowed is that kitchen timer you're using to keep you productive. Email notifications and text messages can wait until you've gotten a big chunk of work done.

No Social Media Sites Allowed

One of the big problems with working online is that we're constantly doing "research" also known as browsing through social media sites and forums. I've wasted plenty of hours going down the rabbit hole and I know you have as well. While there are times to interact on social media sites and there's a time to plop down and watch YouTube videos, now is not that time. Shut down those sites and don't even think about checking in until the work you set out to do is completed.

Work During Off-Times

You are your own boss and that comes with the benefit of being able to make your own hours. If you have small kids that need your attention during the day, carve out a couple of hours after they go to bed to get your most important work done.

If you're still working a full-time job, consider taking a big chunk of your Saturday to work undistracted. Pick the times that work for you and the life around you. Do whatever it takes to get that work done with as few distractions as possible.

Working Smarter - Money Making Principles

Working smarter is also about making the most of your time and efforts financially. It's our way of giving ourselves a raise. Let's look at 3 different ways we can increase the bottom line without working 24/7.

What's Making Money Now?

Track your numbers and take a look at what's making you money right now. Is it selling products on Amazon? Or emailing your newsletter list with an offer? Does your best paying traffic come from Facebook ads? Pinpoint what's making you money. Find your bestselling product, your most profitable source of traffic and your best sales outlet.

The more tracking software you have in place the easier this gets. Install something like Google Analytics and spend some time figuring out how it works and what the data means.

Can You Do More of the Same (or Something Similar?)

For example, if you notice that a blog post you wrote full of tips on how to best use one of your products, start planning and writing Once you know what's working, get creative and figure out how you can do more of the them for your other products.

"Working Smarter" Tips and Principles

If you find that your Pie Recipe book is a good seller on Amazon, come up with a series of other baked goods cookbooks you can publish over the coming year.

Look through each part of your business and find what's working. This can be products, content, emails you wrote or videos you produced. Don't forget about social media. What posts or images got you the most attention? Try to pinpoint why they worked and try doing something similar… or in the case of social media posts and emails, try posting the same thing again every few months.

Find A Reason to contact Your Customers and Prospects

Speaking of email. I don't know about you, but my bottom line increases every time I email my customers and prospects. Look at how often you're emailing now. Can you increase that frequency?

This could be starting a weekly newsletter, or run a seasonal sale. Celebrate a particular holiday, or email them with a "just because" coupon. Look at how other companies and businesses are marketing to you. How can you implement the same ideas?

Come up with a couple of ideas you can try out this month and get to work.

Make A Limited Time Offer

Let's wrap this up with one more money principle. Make your customers and prospects an offer they can't refuse. Bundle a few of your best selling products and offer them at a discount (or add a special bonus). Now here's the important part… make it a limited time offer. Find a reason to make it limited.

Make it customer appreciation week, or if you're creating your offer around Thanksgiving, make it a

"Thank You" sale. Your way of saying thanks for their business.

If you're dealing with physical products, make it a "making room for more stuff" type of sale. The important thing is to put a time limit on your offer and share it with your list. Then sit back and watch the sales roll in.

Chapter 4

Tools to Work Smarter

So far we've talked a lot about how to work smarter. In this next section we'll take a look at some tools that will help you do that. Some of them were mentioned in the previous section already.

Not every tool will be right for each person and business. Give them a try and stick with the ones that work for you.

To Do List Apps

Let's start with my favorite - the to-do list. It's my most used tool when it comes to working smarter... unless you count the spellcheck on my computer. Yes, you can use pen and paper for this, but an app makes your life so much easier. You always have it on you and you can set up recurring tasks to pop up once a day, once a week or once a month.

Google Tasks

This is the simplest one and something that's built into your Google Calendar. It's also available as a Chrome extension. If you're in your Google Calendar all day long, this may be a good solution and something you already have installed.

https://chrome.google.com/webstore/detail/google-tasks-by-google/

Remember The Milk

This is my personal favorite and something I've been using for years. It's available for the web, android and apple devices. It syncs across platforms and has just enough bells and whistles to do what you need it to do without getting overwhelming.
https://www.rememberthemilk.com/services/

Wunderlist

Another App worth looking into is Wunderlist. It also works across all platforms and as an added bonus allows you to share your to-do lists with team members.

Definitely worth checking out if you are working with others on projects.

https://www.wunderlist.com/

There are quite a few other good to-do list apps out there. If you're already using one that works for you, by all means, stick with it. And if the ones suggested don't seem like a good fit, do a little search in the app store and test drive a few others.

Timers

We talked about how important it is to not only know what you're working on but also to set yourself a time limit. That's where countdown timers come in.

Timer On Your Phone

My favorite is the timer on my phone. You may already have a countdown timer built into your phone's clock function. If not, there are plenty of free ones to download from the app store for any smart phone.

Since most of us always have our phones on us, this is a quick and convenient way to use a timer.

Kitchen Timer

If you want to go old school, or if the constant clicking of a kitchen timer is motivation to work faster, consider a kitchen timer. You can pick one up at the Dollar store. Go ahead and grab a couple and leave them around your work spaces.

You want them in easy grabbing reach when you sit down to work.

Focus Booster

A slightly more "high-tech" option is Focus Booster. It's a web-based app that works with your browser. It's based on the Pomodoro technique of working for 25 minutes, then taking a 5-minute break. After a few sets of these you get a longer break.

https://www.focusboosterapp.com/

File Sharing Tools

Working smarter involves being flexible about where you work and what device you work from. You'll also be working with a team and that means you need to share files with other people. As an added bonus, your content will be safer since you have an additional copy of everything you create digitally up in the cloud.

Here are a few file sharing tools I've found helpful in my own business.

Google Docs

Google Docs works very much like a Microsoft Office product, but you can access it anywhere from your browser and your smart phone. All you need is your Gmail login. It's great for editing documents on the fly and sharing them with a team of people.

https://docs.google.com/document

Dropbox

Another personal favorite is Dropbox. It's easy to organize projects in folders that live both on the cloud and on your personal computer (and that of everyone on your team that shares the folder). It's great for collaborations and if you're using a lot of files from multiple computers. It even works on your smartphone, making it easy to attach an important spreadsheet to send to your accountant for example.

www.dropbox.com

SugarSync

I've also heard a lot of good things about SugarSync. It sounds very similar to dropbox but with the added advantage of being able to sync and share file folders you already have on your computer. No need to drop everything into a designated "dropbox" folder first.

https://www.sugarsync.com

"Working Smarter" Tips and Principles

Chapter 5

Share the Wealth and Grow
www.jlnesbitt.com

Chapter 5
How to connect with Clients on LinkedIn

Social networks are a great way to connect with new clients. LinkedIn has over 400 million professionals looking for connections. You can use LinkedIn to build an online presence as well as a professional identity. Anyone who wants to extend their reach and connect with potential clients should be using LinkedIn to do it.

LINKEDIN ACCOUNTS

On LinkedIn, you are a person, first and foremost. When you sign up, you create a free personal account and profile, which includes background and professional information relevant to your potential clients.

LinkedIn offers two types of accounts, free and paid. The main difference between the two is that the paid account does not limit the number or frequency of your actions, like the free account does. With a paid account, you can join more groups, send more messages (InMail) and introductions, view more profile information, see everyone who has viewed your profile, and check references, among other things. Most people begin with a free account and only upgrade if the need arises.

Whether you have a free or paid account, your profile is the foundation you build on. Let's go over the parts of a profile so that you can have your information and details ready to add to each section. It's important to include as much information as possible.

Personal Profile

LinkedIn has set up each personal profile to include information that is similar to a resume. Here, you can include links, images, videos, slide shows, and more. Most of these sections can be repositioned to your liking; however, the headshot is always the first section.

- ✓ **Headshot** – You'll need a professional looking profile photo. You should stick to the professional images that real estate agents are known for, in order to get the best results. But don't worry; you don't have to spend a lot of money for this. Just get someone to take a high-resolution, high-quality headshot or torso shot.

- ✓ **Profile Headline** – Look at profiles. You can see a headline area under each member's name. In this area, write a headline that identifies and describes you. This helps others to find you, even if they don't know you on a personal level...yet.

- ✓ **Summary** – This area should include a well-written summary of your experience, education, and knowledge. Consider using bullet points for easy readability. Use power words to grab attention and include keywords. Keep it professional. Your authority, credibility, and reputation are at stake.

- ✓ **Professional Experience** – Here, enter in each job you've had, or if you're a business owner you can create one job and put all the various things you've accomplished in the list. This part is important because if you worked on a specific project and you want a reference, it's a good idea to list them separately. This allows the people you worked with to link their references to that particular project or task.

- ✓ **Skills & Endorsements** – In this area, check off everything you have experience with including software programs and more. Your connections can then endorse anything that you've said you can do in order to validate your experience.

- ✓ **Education** – This area is where you should include any education you've received. Even if you didn't finish your course of study, include it so that you can connect with fellow alumni. If you received some type of recognition or excelled at something, include the specifics.

- ✓ **Recommendations** – This area is where people can recommend you. LinkedIn provides an easy way to request recommendations from people you've worked with and are connected to. Send personalized, individual requests for the best results. Mass messages tend to be frowned upon by those who receive them and are less likely to take the action you'd prefer.

- ✓ **Groups** – Any groups you join will show up in this section. You don't have to do anything but join. However, try to keep the first 8 to 10 groups related to your target audience or business philosophy/ethics.

- ✓ **Add Media** – You'll notice that under Summary and some other jobs, you'll be allowed to add a document, photo, link, video, or presentation. This is a great way to introduce yourself and help viewers get to know you.

- ✓ **Publications** – If you've written any books or published works, you can list and link to them in this area. This is a wonderful way to show your professionalism. Plus, you might sell a few books.

LinkedIn constantly improves the profile area. Whenever there is a change, take note of it and make use of the improved or added functionality. The more areas you complete the more likely you are to make meaningful connections.

Once you build a solid foundation with your completed personal profile and network by sharing updates, it may be time to add a company page. Let's go over the areas and options associated with a company page.

LinkedIn Company Page

A Company Page allows you to focus on your business in-depth with 4 main sections - home, careers, analytics, and notifications. It is a great option for business owners. You can promote the page in different ways and look at page stats. You can list your products or services and give updates through LinkedIn from your blog. As long as you have a business name, and a business email address you can create your company page.

- ✓ Overview – This is where you'll add your company name and a company description. Think very hard about the description. You can use up to

2000 characters. If you're not sure how to write a company profile, you can hire a copywriter to help you get the wording right.

✓ **Designated Admins** – You can add LinkedIn connections as admins for your page. This helps you create a like-minded team of experts while the connections and exposure helps everyone involved.

✓ **Direct Sponsored Content Posters** – If anyone you're connected to wants to post content on your behalf, you can list them here.

- ✓ **Image** – This is like a banner or cover image. You need to upload the image at the right size for this area.

- ✓ **Logo** – If you have a business logo, add it here. You want your business or company logo to be simple, original, versatile, and easily recognizable.

- ✓ **Company Specialties** – This is the area to make your experience shine so you can get noticed. Include specialties for anything that you do, even if you're not doing it as a main source of income, unless you're not interested in doing it anymore.

"Working Smarter" Tips and Principles

- ✓ **Featured Group** – If you created a LinkedIn group or you are an admin for another group, you can add up to three groups to this page with the free account.

- ✓ **Engagement** – You can share updates by linking to a blog post or video. The content you share here will be shared with your followers on their feed.

- ✓ **Analytics** – This important area allows you to check how your content is performing and how you're building relationships.

- ✓ **Today's Social Actions** – This area of your company page

Share the Wealth and Grow
www.jlnesbitt.com

shows the actions you've done today to make an impact and connect to others. In addition, if your company is mentioned by anyone it will show up here.

With a company page, you can also create career pages to help potential employees get info about your brand, see small business resources, or showcase a page for just one product, service, or brand.

Tips to Connecting with Clients

Whether you are just getting started on LinkedIn or you are renewing your focus, you want to take advantage of the opportunities available to you. While we mentioned the company page previously, many people just use their profiles and the basic account options. For this reason, we will focus on connecting using the basic account and options.

Many of the tips and strategies can also be applied to a company page, as is. However, some may need a slight adjustment to be more effective.

Making Your LinkedIn Profile Work for You

There are a few best practices that you should be aware of when creating a LinkedIn profile. If you pay attention to what you're doing, LinkedIn can be very lucrative for you when it comes to finding new clients and maintaining relationships with current ones.

- **Know Your Why** – If you don't know why you're starting the profile, then you should not do it yet. But if you know that you want to attract your specific audience and why, then go for it. If you don't know your purpose, it can be hard to stay focused.

CHAPTER 6

It's Better "TO OWN" HALF a watermelon than a whole grape"!!!

A short story!!!

COMMON SENSE LEADERSHIP & WEALTH CREATION SKILLS

It's better "to own" one-half of a watermelon than to own a whole grape!

"Working Smarter" Tips and Principles

For a modern high-tech example of this principle, I remember the PBS series " Triumph of the Nerds ". It was a 6 hr. mini/series about 3 computer GIANTS and their key players Microsoft, Apple and IBM. When IBM came into the PC computer business world. There was very little competition. The main focus was on products for the office, not for the home.

However, IBM contracted with Microsoft to design and build the DOS system.

Bill Gates of Microsoft made one of the greatest [financially rewarding] decisions in business history. His decision was to create a system that would run on almost any computer. Microsoft licensed IBM and many other competitors to use his system on their computers. Bill Gates did not try to corner the computer market. Instead he chose to have a small piece of every computer sold.

IBM chose to use another strategy by keeping its machine components to itself. Around the same time Steve Jobs created the Apple. It was a great machine. Easier to operate that the IBM and its clones. Like IBM, Apple would not license any of its engineering or technology. So software was limited. However, software for DOS was available almost anywhere. When Windows was released it was a tremendous blow to IBM and Apple. And Bill Gates became the richest man in the world by using " COMMON CENTS AND SHARING THE WEALTH ".

"Working Smarter" Tips and Principles

IBM closed plants and had to lay off over 80,000 people. It did not choose to share the wealth. IBM suffered greatly along with the employees that were laid off. But IBM is still today a major player in the business world today. Apple with Steve Jobs Leadership, came back and is a giant in the communication Industry today.

" I had rather have 1% of the efforts of 100 men than to have 100% of the efforts of 1 man"   J Paul Getty

     We are all taught to share. When I was a child playing in the sand box. Which was a long time ago for, the old man Jim. The child that shared their toys always had the most friends. The child that tried to keep all the toys in their corner was alone and had no friends. We know that sharing is right.

Share the Wealth and Grow
www.jlnesbitt.com

Yet as we grow older we try to develop our independence, refusing to share with others.

As children we depend on our parents. They tell us what to do and take care of us. When we become adults many people find the same security. They belong to a union that helps them, or they have a boss that tells them what to do. Some people are not happy with this position but they tolerate it because it gives them security.

As we grow we become increasingly independent. Remember when you were a teenager. You got a job spent more time on your own and away from home. In the work place the same thing happens. Some people want to open their own business. Control their own destiny

People in the independent stage must make a choice. They can remain independent, OWNING A WHOLE GRAPE., or they can choose to move into the interdependence stage of life. In the interdependence stage people become replaceable and as they share the wealth and grow in their business. They have a freedom in life that can change their lifestyle. However, this requires great personal growth. You are not responsible for every detail. Interdependence gives you the freedom to concentrate on the big picture, your Dream. You can grow your business and have time
and financial freedom to enjoy the life style you have only dreamed about.

I have observed that highly independent people have a hard time depending on others. Independent people cannot be duplicated.

Share the Wealth and Grow
www.jlnesbitt.com

Interdependent people understand the limitations of being independent.

However interdependent people have shared the wealth, by sharing their skills and knowledge and duplicating their success in others. They understand the message in J Paul Getty's famous quote. " I HAD RATHER HAVE 1 % OF THE EFFORTS OF 100 MEN THAN TO HAVE 100% OF THE EFFORTS OF 1 MAN"

Interdependence does not mean that we lose our individuality. It means that individuals work together to achieve their own mutual benefits.

Individual rewards are not dependent upon the work of the group. It's like this, you will reap what you sow. Each person's rewards are in proportion to their input and their own efforts.

As I said, highly effective people are working in networks. In a network individuals provide each other with help so that personal goals can be met. In a network, a small business, a company network system or a network of volunteers. For example, the [CAP] Civil Air Patrol, Church prayer groups or chains as they are referred to some time. In these examples each individual is interdependent on others. Networks are everywhere. In my opinion the greatest example of networking is Christianity. Jesus Christ took 12 men, that built a network of Christians that still has a positive effect on our world today. I am blessed to say I am a part of that worldwide network.

"Working Smarter" Tips and Principles

I do not believe that it is possible to build a large business or group while working independently. This strategy will only carry you so far.

Interdependence makes you replaceable and your efforts can be duplicated. This allows for your wealth to increase. By allowing each person to contribute and receive rewards proportionally.

COMMONSENSE WEALTH SAYS!!!

Build your network and receive benefits produced by others. Who are working for your success, while they achieve their own success.

In fact, I believe we can surpass the advice of J. Paul Getty and receive not just 1 % of the efforts of 100 men. but

it is possible to receive 1 % on the efforts of 1000's of men and women. This is the kind of duplication that has the potential to produce tremendous wealth. We will be sharing the wealth by duplicating our success in others.

Share the Wealth and Grow
www.jlnesbitt.com

"Working Smarter" Tips and Principles

> "Some smart individuals have found a way to generate "RESIDUAL" income. This is income that continues to come in even if you don't continue to work"
>
> *James Leroy Nesbitt*

WORKING SMARTER CHECKLIST

What Is Working Smarter?

- ✓ Working smarter means working more efficiently and getting things done in less time

- ✓ Working smarter means picking high priority tasks

- ✓ Working smarter means delegating some tasks

- ✓ Working smarter means automating some tasks

- ✓ Working smarter means cutting out distractions

✓ **Working smarter means focusing on money making tasks**

Working Smarter – Efficiency Principles

- ✓ To do lists are your friend
- ✓ Set yourself time limits - use that kitchen timer
- ✓ Work 25 minutes, take a 5-minute break
- ✓ Work hard, then play

Working Smarter - Priority Principles

- ✓ Get the big picture - map it out
- ✓ Tweak the to do list
- ✓ Work on your top 3 tasks first
- ✓ Save the easy stuff for downtime

Working Smarter - Delegating Principles

- ✓ Is this the best use of your time?
- ✓ Can someone else do it better and faster?
- ✓ Start to outsource
- ✓ Hire a VA

Working Smarter – Automation Tips

- ✓ Is there an easier way?

- ✓ Is there a tool / app for that? Look at what others in your niche or business model are automating

Working Smarter – Tips to Cut Out Distractions

- ✓ Shut the door

- ✓ Turn off alerts, alarms and your phone

- ✓ No social media sites allowed

- ✓ Work during off-times

Working Smarter - Making Money

"Working Smarter" Tips and Principles

- ✓ What's making money now?
- ✓ Can you do more of the same (or something similar?)
- ✓ Find a reason to contact your customers and prospects
- ✓ Make a limited time offer

Conclusion

Are you ready to start working smarter instead of harder? You have the strategies and tools you need to work fewer hours and get more done in the time you spend at your desk.

We talked about a lot of different "TIPS & PRINCIPLES" in this book. Don't let the sheer volume of information overwhelm you. Start by implementing just a few things that sound interesting or something you can quickly give a try.

"Working Smarter" Tips and Principles

If you don't do anything else right away, please grab a piece of paper and a pen and make out a short to-do list of things you want to get done tomorrow. Start there and then work your way through the remaining principles or tips.

Some of them will work well for you, others may not. Don't feel like this is written in stone. Use what's working for you and making you more productive.

Share the Wealth and Grow
www.jlnesbitt.com

Make it a point to come back to this book from time to time and revisit these ideas. Just because outsourcing isn't the right thing for you right now, doesn't mean it won't be just the thing you need to move forward a few months from now. The same goes for some of the other principles that may not be a good fit for you at the moment.

Work smart and make every hour count!

A QUOTE TO REMEMBER

"I refuse to live a life that is less than what I am capable of living and short of what GOD created me to do."

Steve Fisher

www.stevefisher.com

Share the Wealth and Grow
www.jlnesbitt.com

"Working Smarter" Tips and Principles

"How to work less and earn more Money"

Working Smarter is the first book of a series

Look for the next Book soon

Send James an email and he will send you an update when the next book.

"Working Smarter the Business Mindset" will be published. mailto:worklessearmore@outloook.com

SHARE THE WEALTH AND GROW!!!

"The Wealth we need to share is the knowledge and skills we have learned in life by duplicating our success in others"

James Leroy Nesbitt

Have a Blessed and Prosperous Future!!!

"The Joy is in the Journey"

James Leroy Nesbit

Share the Wealth and Grow
www.jlnesbitt.com

"Working Smarter" Tips and Principles

I sincerely hope that you will achieve the recognition of

A TOP MONEY EARNER

in the business arena of your choice.

Remember to make every hour count. "Working Smarter"

Don't waste time! You can make more money but you can't make more time.

Share the Wealth and Grow
www.jlnesbitt.com

"Working Smarter" Tips and Principles

To your Success

James Leroy Nesbitt

"Some smart individuals have found a way to generate "RESIDUAL" income. This is income that continues to come in even if you don't continue to work"

James Leroy Nesbitt

"The Wealth we need to Share is the Knowledge and Skills we have Learned by Duplicating our SUCCESS in OTHERS"

James Leroy Nesbitt

Share the Wealth and Grow
www.jlnesbitt.com

"Working Smarter" Tips and Principles

"Don't waste time!! Make every hour count. You can earn more money but you can't create more time"

James Leroy Nesbitt

Share the Wealth and Grow
www.jlnesbitt.com

"Working Smarter" Tips and Principles

NOTES

"Working Smarter" Tips and Principles

NOTES

"Working Smarter" Tips and Principles

NOTES

"Working Smarter" Tips and Principles

NOTES

"Working Smarter" Tips and Principles